Manga Doodles

Buster Books

Illustrated by Yuriko Yano

First published in Great Britain in 2009 by Buster Books,
an imprint of Michael O'Mara Books Limited,
9 Lion Yard, Tremadoc Road,
London SW4 7NQ

A CIP catalogue record for this book is available
from the British Library.

ISBN: 978-1-906082-70-3

2 4 6 8 10 9 7 5 3 1

Printed and bound in Italy by L.E.G.O.

Create a cool castle.

Fill the sky with dragons and riders.

Friends or foes?

What world have we landed in?

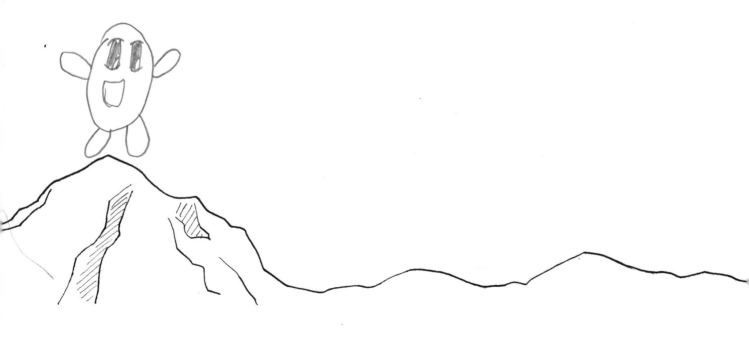

Pirates ahoy!

Complete the magical story.

AHA!

WHAT A GREAT WAY TO GET THE SORCERER BACK FOR THIS ...

4

HE SWOOPED BACK TO THE CAVE AND ...

5

... MAGICALLY TRANSFORMED THE SORCERER.

KAPOW!

6

What is he lifting?

What must he fight?

The best ice cream ever.

Finish her superstar outfit.

Escape from the fairground.

Fill the sky with arrows.

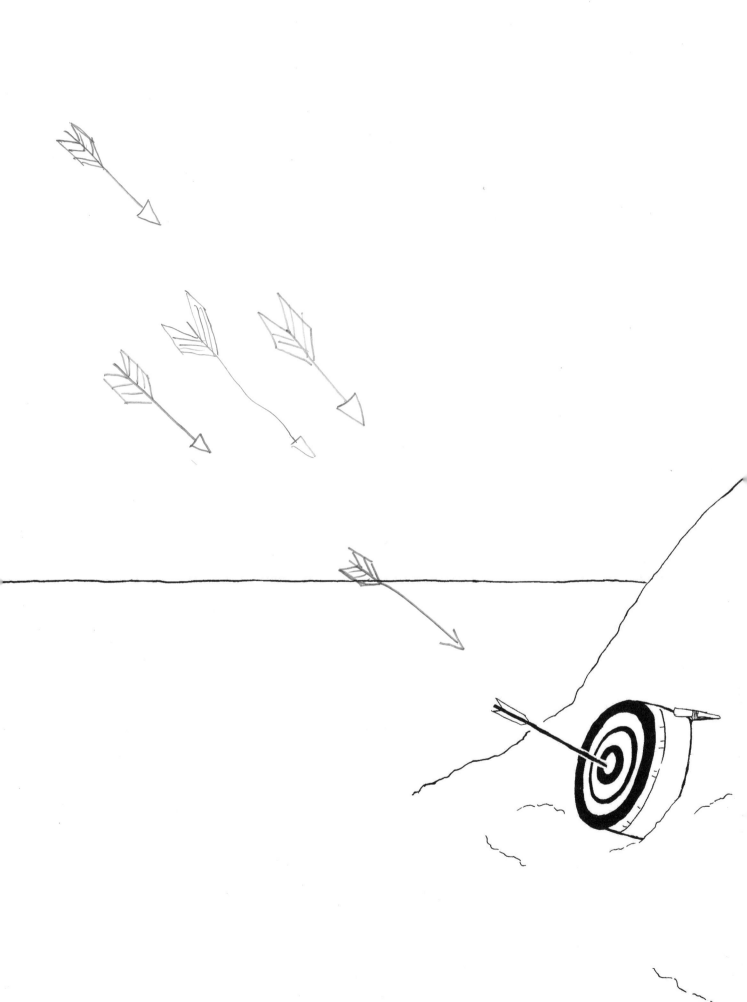

Fill the plates with sushi.

What an astonishing view.

Prepare a magical feast.

Land of the giants.

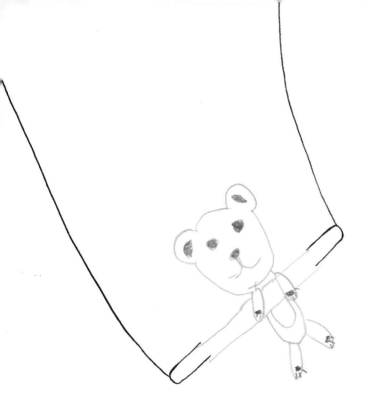

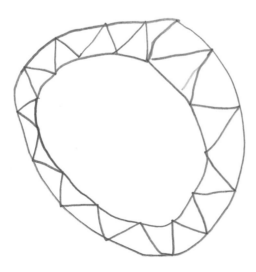

Catch me!

Look out!

Magical fancy dress.

Complete the map and find the hidden treasure.

What will he take on his trip?

Sweet dreams.

Who is the hero fighting?

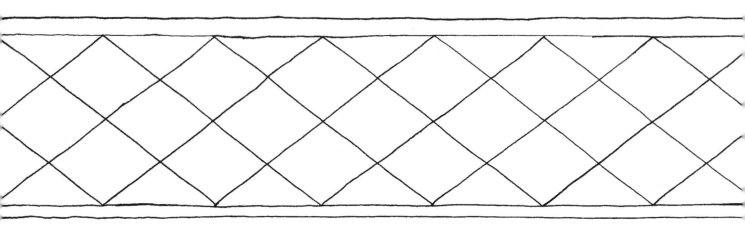

Give them some instruments.

Who lives upstairs?

Glorious fireworks.

What are they scared of?

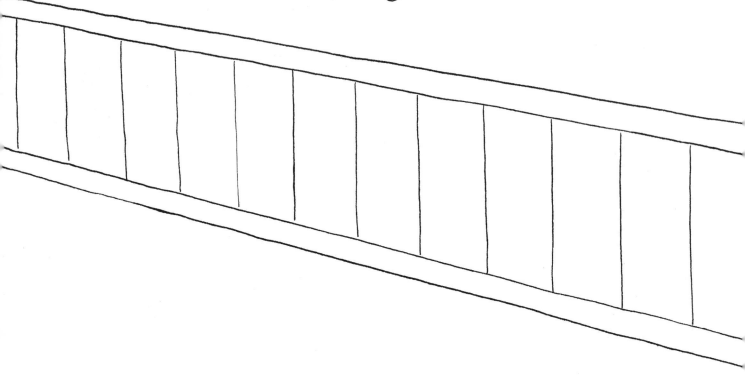

Fill the chest with treasure.

Build the best sandcastle ever.

Hocus pocus!

To the rescue!

OH NO

HELP!

WHAT'S THAT?

1

2

THE BOY FELL AND FELL ...

3

Complete the superhero story.

LET'S FLY TO
THE RESCUE.

THERE'S NO
TIME TO LOSE,
CAPTAIN CAT.

THEY SPED TOWARDS
THE MOUNTAIN ...

5

4

... AND SAVED HIM.

6

WHAT A RELIEF!

Create an amazing aeroplane.

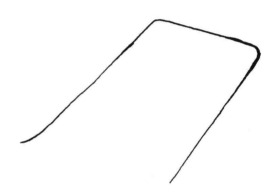

Catch of the day.

Who is she rescuing?

Who is in the bubbles?

Fill the flower garden.

What a wonderful tree house.

Where are they heading?

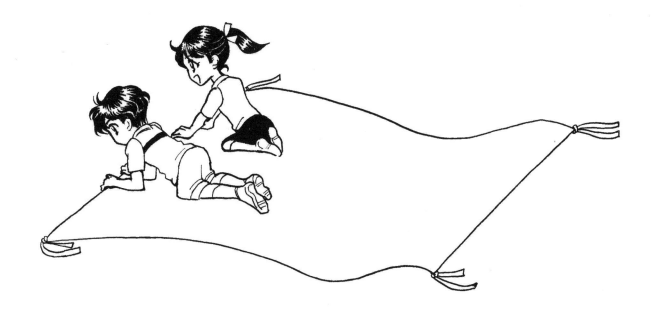

Fill the woods with wildlife.

Super samurai.

Where are the
others hiding?

Lost in Toyland.

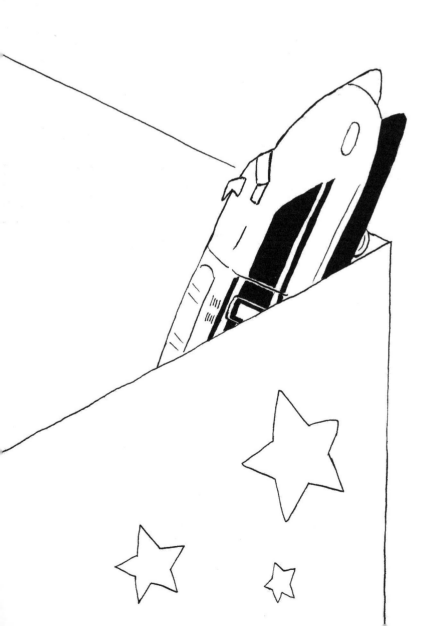

Who's hiding in the treetops?

Show their facial expressions.

What has the class magician conjured?

What have they found in the desert?

All the sweets in the world.

Wild wave!

Lost in space.

Draw her portrait.

Ouch! Good throw.

A magical fairy spell.

What is sleeping in the cave?

A spectacular underwater palace.

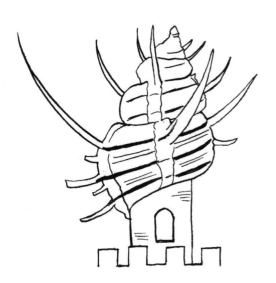

Complete the city skyline.

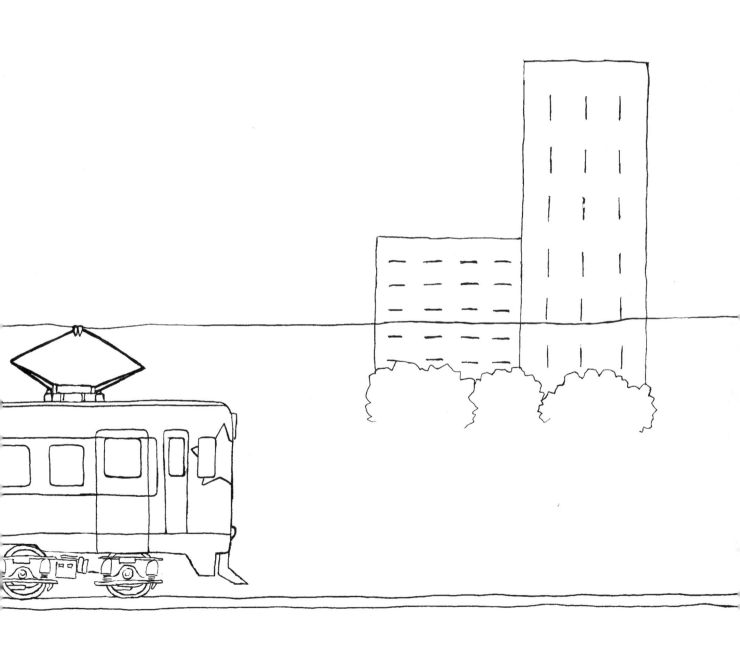

What has he conjured?

What is heading for the trap?

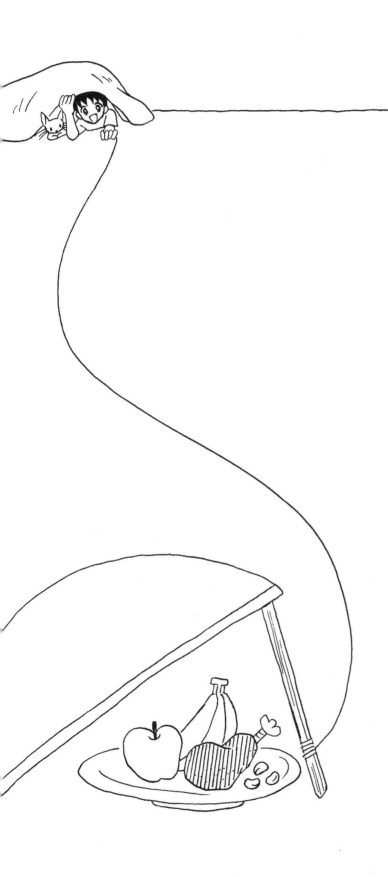

Complete their cool T-shirts!

Who is swimming in the magical lake?

Show them the way home.

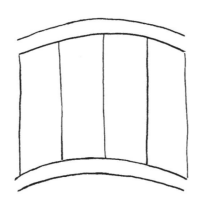

Who is riding the dolphin?

What a cool campsite.

Fantastic future world.

Who is invited to the picnic?

Who is he carrying?

Complete and decorate their outfits and equipment.

Complete the daring rescue.

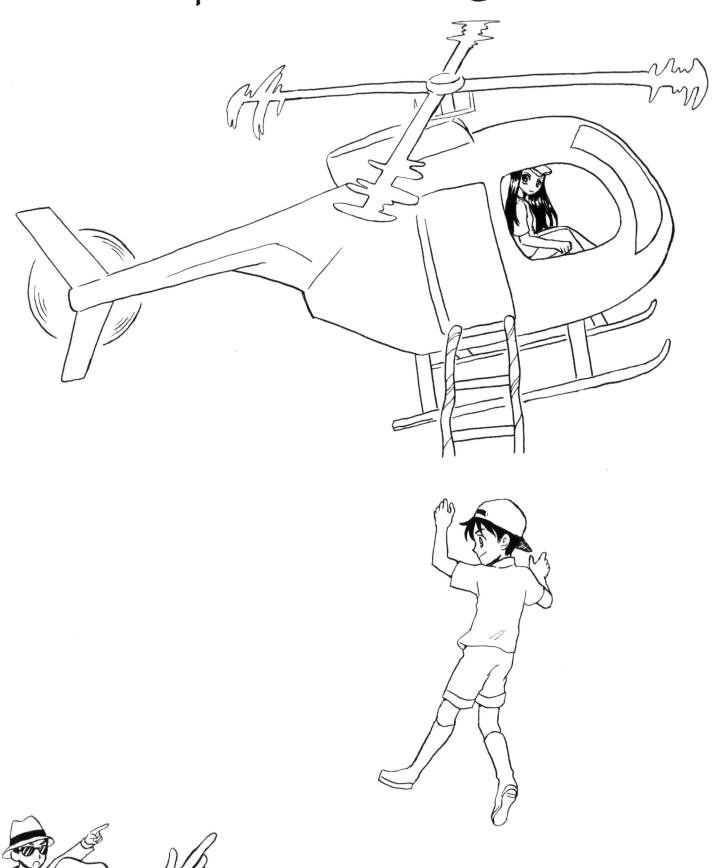

Who is trapped in the ice?

Fill the sky with witches and wizards.

Get them ready for the game.

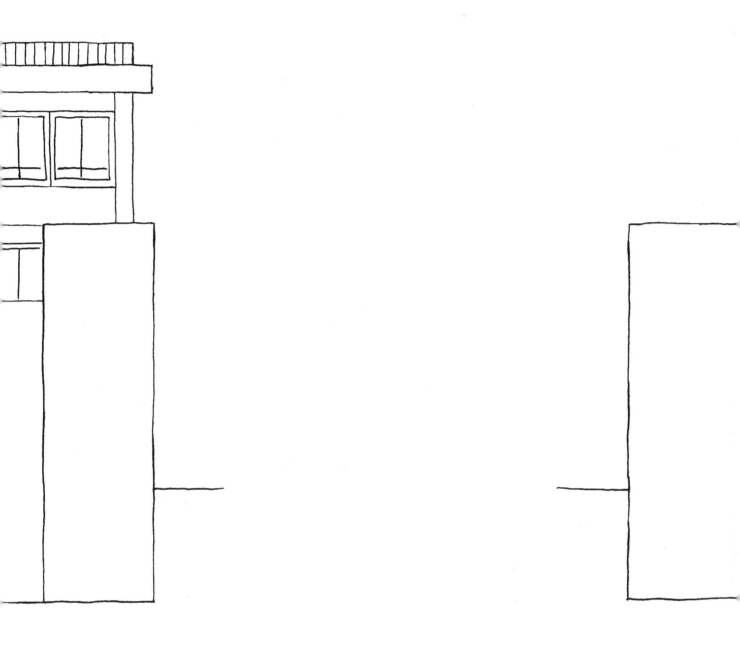

What are they escaping from?

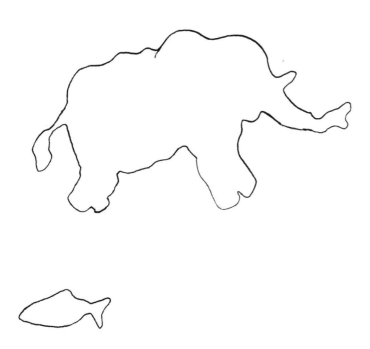

What can they see in the clouds?

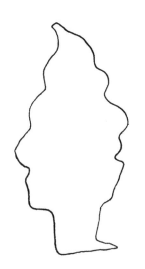

Eat up.

Make her magical plants grow.

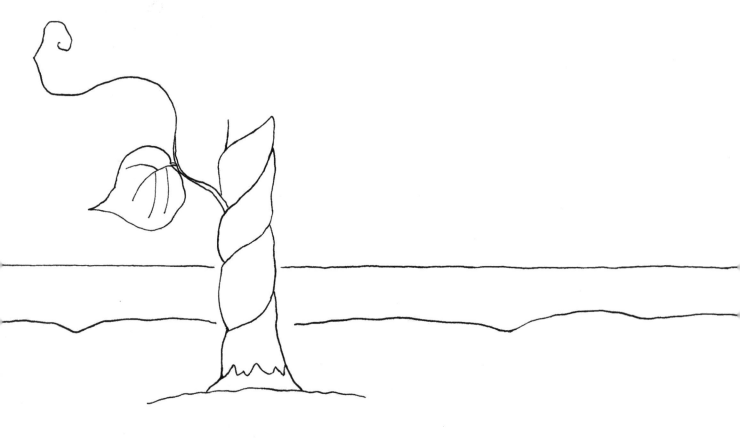

What is hatching?

What gift will he buy?

1 ONLY YOU CAN TAKE THE SCROLL SAFELY TO THE TEMPLE.

2 I WILL TAKE EXCELLENT CARE OF IT.

YOUR POWERS WILL PROTECT IT.

3 SHE SAW HER RIVALS.

Complete the adventure story.

MAYBE I CAN CHANGE THEM INTO ...

... MICE!

SHE REACHED THE TEMPLE AND GAVE THE SCROLL TO THE MASTER.

6

Watch out for the sea monster!

Decorate her costume.